Date Due

SEP 2 4 2015			

BRODART, CO.   Cat. No. 23-233-003   Printed in U.S.A.

HENRY
DAVID
THOREAU

HENRY DAVID THOREAU

American Naturalist

by
Peter Anderson

A First Book
Franklin Watts
A Division of Grolier Publishing
New York / London / Hong Kong / Sydney
Danbury, Connecticut

Cover photograph copyright ©: North Wind Picture Archives; Archive Photos (insert).

Photographs copyright ©: North Wind Picture Archives: pp. 2, 8, 26, 37, 44, 49, 51;
Bettmann Archive: pp. 11, 17, 21, 35, 53, 56; Walden Pond State Reservcation: pp. 13
(Roland Robbins), 19 (Denise Morrissey), 32, 39; Concord Museum: p. 23; Society for the
Preservation of New England Antiquities: pp. 24; Reprinted from *Discovery at Walden*,
Barnstead & Son, 1947: p. 30; Archive Photos: p. 42; Concord Free Public Library:
pp. 47, 55, 58.

Library of Congress Cataloging-in-Publication Data

Anderson, Peter, 1956—
Henry David Thoreau : American naturalist / by Peter Anderson.
    p. cm. — (A First book)
Includes bibliographical references (p.) and index.
ISBN 0-531-20206-2
    1. Thoreau, Henry David, 1817–1862—Juvenile literature
2. Naturalists—United States—Biography—Juvenile literature.
3. Conservationists—United States—Biography—Juvenile literature.
    [1. Thoreau, Henry David, 1817–1862. 2. Naturalists.
    3. Conservationists.] I. Title. II. Series.
QH31.M9A54 1995
333.7'2'092—dc20
[B]
                                                                95-3225 CIP AC

CONTENTS

HENRY DAVID THOREAU

Concord, Massachusetts, as it appeared in the mid-1800s; the church on the right is where Henry David Thoreau was baptized.

CHAPTER ONE

TALK OF THE TOWN

A river, with its waterfalls and meadows, a lake, a hill, a cliff or individual rocks, a forest, ancient trees standing singly. . . . If the inhabitants of a town were wise, they would seek to preserve these things. . . . For such things educate far more than any hired teachers or preachers.

—Henry David Thoreau

They often saw him out walking. He was likely dressed in stout shoes and homespun coat and trousers, thick enough to withstand the scrub oaks and brambles that covered the countryside around the village. Tucked under his arm was the old music book that he used for pressing plants. If he ran out of pages, he stored extra plants underneath his straw hat.

It was said that he traveled the countryside like a fox. Sometimes he emerged from a thicket only long enough to cross a road. Then he disappeared into the brush again. Farmers occasionally caught a glimpse of him as he followed a cow trail down the far side of a hedgerow. Then he wandered off into the woods.

There were those in town who had seen him sit by a pond for hours just to listen to the frogs croak. Others claimed he had spent an entire day by the river watching ducks hatch. Someone saw him admiring a willow tree one day and mistook him for a drunkard in a trance. Most of his neighbors were never quite sure what Henry David Thoreau was up to. They just knew that he liked to walk.

In 1845, Concord, Massachusetts, was a good place to walk. Two streams met above town to form the Concord River, which rolled past broad meadows and farms, past swamps teeming with fish and turtles and waterbirds, past tree-lined streets with well-kept homes. It meandered past the shops that surrounded the village green, past the site of an old mill dam where people gathered for news and trade. As a boy growing up in the heart of town, Henry

Thoreau's birthplace in Concord, Massachusetts

liked to pull on the oars of an old rowboat, skimming like a water spider down the dark river.

On those days when he chose to go afoot, it was only a matter of hopping a fence, maybe cutting across a meadow or two, and Henry could breathe in the moist scent of the pine woods that rimmed the village. In ancient times, slow-moving ice flows called glaciers had shaped the rolling hills around Concord. Looking west from the highest of these hills, Henry could see several isolated mountains, part of the great Appalachian range that stretched from Georgia to Maine. Below him were some of the many ponds that dotted the woodlands around the village.

It was near the shore of one such pond that Henry would decide to build a cabin. Cupped in the wooded hills about a mile outside of Concord, Walden Pond had long been one of Henry's favorite places. He cherished the memory of a visit to the pond with his grandmother in 1822 when he was five years old. He remembered walking with her through sunlight and shadows underneath the tall pines. He remembered looking out over the still blue water.

Twenty-three years later in 1845, Henry returned to Walden Pond. As he began to cut down the pine trees he would need for his cabin, news of

Henry Thoreau loved the area around
Walden Pond and built a cabin there.

his intentions drifted into the conversations of villagers down by the old mill dam.

One of the villagers referred to Thoreau as the "damned rascal" who had set fire to some woods near town the previous spring. Henry had been out fishing on the Sudbury River with another young man from Concord. As they were cooking up their catch on a tree stump beside the river, a gust of wind had whirled their fire into some dry grass. Flames raced through the grass and into the briars. By the time they had been able to round up the help needed to put out the fire, the blaze had blackened some of Henry's favorite woods.

Such an unfortunate accident only added to the opinion held by some Concord residents that Henry Thoreau was a less than useful citizen. It wasn't because of his family—they were respectable people. His father had a pencil-making business. His hospitable mother always took in boarders. It wasn't for lack of education. After all, Henry had graduated from Harvard.

True, Henry and his brother had run a private school for several years. But after the school closed down, Henry rarely worked, it seemed, except for odd jobs now and then. Occasionally he worked with his father making pencils. He had hired on as a handyman for a well-known local family. But as far as many of his neighbors were concerned, such work was hardly suited to a Harvard graduate. To them, Henry Thoreau was just a well-educated loafer who wore frumpy clothes, liked to walk, and preferred the company of pine trees to people. Whatever he intended to do out at Walden Pond, they figured, probably wouldn't amount to much.

A FAITHFUL FRIEND

If a man does not keep pace with his companions, perhaps it is because he hears a different drummer. Let him step to the music which he hears, however measured or far away.

—Henry David Thoreau

Not everyone in Concord took such a dim view of Henry David Thoreau. Among those who saw him in a more positive light, was a famous writer and philosopher named Ralph Waldo Emerson.

What others described as loafing, Emerson recognized as an unusual devotion to the study of nature. Even though he had written on the impor-

Ralph Waldo Emerson was one of early America's greatest
philosophers. As they shared their love of nature, Emerson
and Thoreau developed a lasting friendship.

tance of appreciating nature, Emerson had never taken the time to observe it as thoroughly as young Thoreau had. To walk with Henry was to see the forest through a new set eyes. For Emerson, Henry became a guide of sorts, one who named the plants, described the animals, and delighted in eating acorns, huckleberries, and wild apples.

"It was a pleasure and privilege to walk with him," Emerson would later write of Thoreau. "He knew the country like a fox or a bird and passed through it freely by paths of his own. He knew every track in the snow or on the ground, and what creature had taken this path before him . . . His memory was a photographic register of all he saw and heard."

As Emerson would learn from Thoreau, so Thoreau had learned from Emerson. Even before meeting the famous philosopher, Henry had read many of his writings. While Henry had developed a knack for observing the details of nature, Emerson preferred to contemplate its meaning. Those willing to open up to the wonders of nature, Emerson believed, would find great rewards. To observe and understand nature, he suggested, was like reading the writing of God.

Emerson's words rang true for Henry. He too believed that there was far more to nature than most people took the time to see. Henry's ambition

The woods near Walden Pond in autumn

was to immerse himself in the natural world and describe what he saw in his writing. Such was the work of a naturalist who also yearned to be a poet. Emerson's writings encouraged such an approach to nature.

The two men first became acquainted shortly after Henry began to keep a journal. In the pages of his journal, Henry recorded the observations that he made daily while tramping through the countryside around Concord. And he continued to write the kind of poems and essays that he had recently written as a student of literature at Harvard.

One day, his sister Helen read some of Henry's writings. She passed them on to Emerson's sister-in-law, thinking that Henry and the famous philosopher shared many of the same ideals. Arrangements were soon made for the two men to meet.

Emerson was impressed with Henry. If anyone had taken his ideas to heart, it seemed as though this young man had. Before long, Henry had become a regular guest at the Emerson home, joining the other writers and thinkers who gathered there periodically to discuss the topics of the day.

For a young man recently graduated from Harvard, the invitation to join this group of thinkers was an exciting opportunity, especially in a small village such as Concord. Henry had no trouble keeping

A young Henry Thoreau

up with the conversations. "I delight much in my young friend," Emerson wrote in his diary after one such gathering in February 1838. Henry "seems to have as free and erect a mind as any I have ever met."

Emerson's admiration and support could not have come at a better time in his "young friend's" life. Emerson inspired Henry to pursue his true passions—nature and literature—even though he often needed to look elsewhere to make a living. One attempt at making a living had been the private school he ran with his brother, John, for several years. But after a bout with tuberculosis, John was no longer able to teach, and the school closed down. John would never fully recover. On January 11, 1842, he died from a painful tetanus infection.

Henry was badly shaken by his brother's death. He had always looked to his family for the friendship that had often eluded him elsewhere. After a boyhood spent hunting and fishing and paddling the river, John and Henry had been especially close. It was John who first taught his younger brother how to identify birds. And it was John who would later join Henry on a canoe journey up the Concord and Merrimack rivers. Around that same time, they both fell in love with a young woman named Ellen Sewall, they both proposed marriage, and they both were turned down. Such a rejection had been

Henry's brother, John Thoreau. John's death from a tetanus infection saddened Henry deeply.

After the Thoreau brothers closed their school, Ralph Waldo Emerson hired Henry to take care of his estate.

painful for Henry, but it was nothing compared to the loss of a brother.

In the period of grief that followed, Henry found solace in nature and family. He grew closer to the Emersons with whom he now lived. Several months after the Thoreaus had closed their school, Emerson had hired Henry as a live-in handyman. In exchange for his room and board, Henry was to look after the grounds of the Emerson estate and help out around the household. Such an arrangement allowed Henry to pursue his interests without much worry as far as making a living was concerned.

Under such circumstances, Emerson hoped that Henry's writing would flourish. As editor of a magazine called *The Dial*, Emerson gladly published some of Henry's poems and essays. But if Henry was going to establish himself as a writer, he would also need to publish elsewhere. So in the spring of 1843, Emerson arranged for Henry to take a tutoring job near New York City. And he provided Henry with letters of introduction so that he could get acquainted with other writers and editors.

The new situation was agreeable enough. Henry liked Emerson's brother William, whose children he tutored. And his job left him plenty of time to explore the streets and offices of New York, as he attempted to break into print. He was able to

In the 1840s, New York City was a bustling, crowded place. It did not take long for Henry to miss the woods and rivers around Concord.

sell a few articles, but for the most part, his efforts to sell himself as a writer were met with rejections. "My best will not tempt the rats," he wrote of his encounters with New York editors. "They are too well fed."

Meanwhile, he was growing tired of New York City. "It must have a very bad influence on children," he wrote home in a letter, "to see so many human beings at once, — mere herds of men." Clearly it was having a bad influence on Henry Thoreau, and he began to long for his home: "My thoughts revert to those dear hills and that river which so fills up the world to its brim."

So Henry returned to Concord, less accomplished than he might have hoped. But there had been a few successes. And his experience of the city had reassured him that he was a fortunate man indeed to have grown up in a country village such as Concord. Still, there was the question of making a living. If he couldn't support himself as a writer, what were his options? Was there a way to make a living that wouldn't interfere with his writing and nature study?

For the time being, answers may have eluded Henry, but the questions kept on coming. What were the necessities of life? Could he live a simpler life without many of the comforts and luxuries that others considered necessary? How much money did he really need?

In the spring of 1845, as Henry Thoreau grappled with questions such as these, he received a letter from Emerson who was working for a newspaper in New York City. Henry's old friend made an interesting proposal. He described a piece of land that he had recently purchased out on the shores of Walden Pond. "Go out upon that land," Emerson suggested to Henry, and "build yourself a hut."

CHAPTER THREE

A CABIN BY THE POND

Sometimes . . . I sat in my sunny doorstep from sunrise till noon, rapt in a revery, in undisturbed solitude and stillness, while the birds sang or flitted noiseless through the house, until by the sun falling in at my west window, or the noise of some traveler's wagon on the distant highway, I was reminded of the lapse of time. I grew in those seasons like corn in the night.
— Henry David Thoreau

The dark ice that still covered most of the pond was melting fast. A few bird songs, the steady whack of an ax, and the cracking of branches as the tall pines fell—these were the sounds heard out at Walden in

Thoreau writes in his journal at his Walden cabin.

late March 1845 as Henry Thoreau began to build his cabin.

In exchange for the privilege of building on Emerson's land, Henry agreed to clear out a field of briars. It seemed a good arrangement for both men, especially for Henry who Emerson believed to be a "promising if still unfruitful thinker." Just as some forest plants grow better with less sunlight, perhaps Henry's talents would blossom with less exposure to the distractions of village life. Walden Pond was only a mile or so from town, close enough to keep up with friends and family. But for Henry it was also far enough away so that he could find the solitude he needed to concentrate on his writing and studies.

If self-reliance and a simple life offered solutions to the puzzle of making a living, what better place to be than Walden Pond? Near the hillside where he built his cabin was a small field where he could grow his own food and perhaps a cash crop, too. And he knew he'd never go hungry living next to a pond full of perch and shiners.

The way Henry Thoreau figured it, there were four "necessaries of life" that no human could do without: shelter, food, clothing, and fuel. Certainly there were a few other tools that would come in handy at Walden—among them a knife,

A modern replica of Thoreau's
cabin on Walden Pond

an ax, a spade, and a wheelbarrow. And there were accessories for his work: a lamplight, stationery, and several books.

Henry once joked that the toolsheds used by railroad workers, wooden boxes about 6 feet (about 2 m) long and 3 feet (1 m) wide often seen along the tracks, were perfectly usable as shelters. "Many a man . . . harassed to death to pay the rent of a larger and more luxurious box," he remarked, "would not have frozen in a box such as this." A house need only be a shelter, Henry argued, not a palace. His own "box" out at Walden Pond was 10 by 15 feet (3 by 4.5 m). It had a closet, a cellar, two windows, and a brick fireplace and was completed in time for his first Walden winter at a cost of $28.12.

It was a simply furnished home, containing a bed, a table, and three chairs — "one for solitude, two for friendship, and three for society," as he put it. His favorite place for entertaining company during the summer was the "outdoor sitting room" in the pine woods behind his cabin where the wind took care of the dusting and sweeping. He preferred to cook outside over a stone-lined firepit using only the simplest of utensils. A lady had offered him a door-mat for wiping his feet, but he declined her offer. The grass by the front door worked perfectly well and never needed shaking.

"I sometimes caught a mess of fish for my dinner," Henry wrote, "and once I went so far as to slaughter a woodchuck which ravaged my bean field . . . and devour him, partly for experiment's sake." It was an experiment, in part because of the woodchuck's "musky flavor," which he never chose to repeat.

For the most part, Henry lived on beans and others vegetables which he grew on 2.5 acres (1 ha) of land beside the pond. The soil was so sandy, one neighboring farmer said it was "good for nothing but to raise cheeping squirrels on." Henry grew a decent crop nevertheless.

Delicacies he preferred such as rice, flour, sugar, and pork—what others might consider common items—he bought for about 27 cents per week.

Clothes were a simple matter. Henry felt that the primary uses of clothes, were after all, to retain heat and cover oneself. It was durability, not appearance, that was important. A thick coat could be had for $5, thick pants for $2, cowhide boots for $1.50, a summer hat for 25¢, and a winter hat for 60¢. The older the clothes, he figured, the better they fit. "No man ever stood the lower in my estimation," Henry said, "for having a patch on his clothes."

As far as fuel for heat and cooking was concerned, Henry gathered stumps from the bean

This section of Walden Pond is called
"Thoreau's Cove." It is located close to
the site of Thoreau's cabin.

field and dead wood from the forest. "Every man looks at his woodpile with a kind of affection," he said. "I loved to have mine before my window." On winter days, the logs warmed him twice, once as he split them with his ax and again as they crackled on the fire.

So it was that Henry Thoreau managed to take care of the necessaries of life at Walden Pond. By doing without many of the comforts that his neighbors in the village were used to, he found new freedom. He determined from his experience at Walden that he need only spend six weeks of every year providing for himself. Occasionally, he took on odd jobs in town to add to his meager savings. On other occasions, he delivered lectures at the Concord Lyceum (an association for concerts and lectures), where villagers gathered periodically to hear talks on various topics.

Henry had plenty of time left to visit with friends and family in town, not to mention the many guests that he entertained at Walden. Neighbors, such as the French woodcutter who liked to eat woodchuck, often stopped by. Farmers couldn't resist offering a suggestion or two as they passed him in his bean field. Young people from the village were able to talk more freely with Henry than they were with their families at home. Visiting Walden became a Concord pastime,

The Concord River today is still a wonderful place
to contemplate the beauty of nature, as it was when
Henry and John Thoreau traveled it by canoe.

not only for those who knew Henry, but also for those who were curious about his activities out there.

Even with all the visiting, Henry still had plenty of time to himself. Each day he wrote in his journal. He often took time to work on what would later become his first book—an account of adventures with his brother John, paddling the Concord and Merrimack rivers. But he spent most of his time outside, immersed in the cycles of the seasons.

On summer mornings, Henry paced back and forth along the furrows of his bean field, leaving barefoot tracks in the dewy sand. As he hoed away the weeds, he left fresh soil around the stem of each bean plant. Summer was a time for "making the earth say beans instead of grass," as he put it. " I came to love my rows, my beans . . . They attached me to the earth and so I got strength."

By September, when the scarlet leaves of the maples danced in the ripples out on Walden Pond, Henry was down by the river gathering wild grapes, out in the fields collecting berries, or back in the woods harvesting chestnuts. Sometimes the best way to gather chestnuts was to climb and shake the trees, much to the dismay of the squirrels and jays who freely voiced their complaints.

As his fire crackled on winter nights, Henry heard the whooping and groaning of the ice as it

Thoreau enjoyed Walden Pond as much in winter
as in any other season.

shifted and settled out on Walden Pond. There were those in Concord who claimed the pond was bottomless. Such claims fired Henry's curiosity. He took it upon himself to map the underside of the frozen pond, dropping a weighted rope through chopped holes to determine its depths. Walden Pond, he discovered, indeed had a bottom, 102 feet (31 m) down at its deepest point. Such a project was typical of Henry's growing interest in collecting scientific data as he observed the natural world. Still, there were plenty of times when he simply let the sights, sounds, smells of the season flow through him like the snowmelt that ran through the meadows in spring. To have the time to watch the spring come in — to hear the first sparrow song, to see the grass burst out on the hillsides, to smell the rich earth as it soaked in moisture, this was true wealth for Henry David Thoreau.

CHAPTER FOUR

THE PIONEER WHO STAYED AT HOME

I wish . . . to derive my satisfactions and inspirations from the commonest events, every-day phenomena, so that what my senses hourly perceive, my daily walk, the conversation of my neighbors, may inspire me, and I may dream of no heaven but that which lies about me.

— Henry David Thoreau

"Our village life would stagnate if it were not for the unexplored forests and meadows which surround it," Thoreau would write in his account of the Walden experience. "We need the tonic of wildness." Having tasted a certain wildness out at Walden,

A view from Maine's Mount Katahdin

Henry yearned for an experience of even wilder lands, of lands like those in western America which humans had yet to settle. In August 1846, he sought out such a place in the woods of northern Maine.

Leaving his fellow travelers behind, Henry climbed along a rocky spine of Mount Katahdin, the highest mountain in Maine. The summit was hidden in the clouds that day. But when the wind blew, windows of blue sky occasionally opened. And they revealed, as he made his way back down the mountain, miles and miles of wild lakes and woodlands, unmarred by clearings or houses. Wrote Henry: "It did not look as if a solitary traveler had cut so much as a walking-stick there."

Such wildness called to Henry's adventurous spirit, just as it called to thousands of American pioneers who were heading west at that time to carve out new lives on the frontier. In later years, Henry would return to the woods of Maine, and he would explore the forests of Canada as well as the outer reaches of Cape Cod, but it was Concord that he mostly yearned to know.

Many of his Concord neighbors who shared his homeland wondered what, if anything, Henry Thoreau had accomplished by living out at Walden Pond for two years. "My purpose in going to Walden pond was not to live cheaply . . . ," Henry

When Thoreau lived in the Emerson house, he no doubt spent countless hours reading and writing in the library.

wrote, "but to transact some private business with the fewest obstacles." Just what was that private business, his critics might have wondered?

Certainly, he had written a lot. He had completed his first book, which would soon be published, and he had written hundreds of journal pages that would provide the material for his second. He had also proven to himself that he was capable, indeed anyone was capable, of living a comfortable life without many of the things others considered necessities. But perhaps his most important discovery was that a simple life, devoted to the study of nature and a love of language, was enough to bring him a deep sense of joy. It was this sense of joy that convinced him he was on the right track, despite the doubts and criticisms of his fellow villagers.

Why then did he leave Walden Pond? Perhaps he had learned all the lessons that living at Walden had to teach him. Perhaps he realized that he could carry on a simple life even if he lived in town.

As much as Henry enjoyed the freedom of his solitude, he had never given up his contact with friends and family, nor had he intended to. An invitation to live with the Emersons again promised a sense of belonging that only life with a family could offer. Before leaving for a lecture tour of England, Emerson had asked Henry to take care of his house and family. Emerson's wife, Lidian, was bedridden with an illness and would need some help. Henry was glad to oblige.

Over the years, Henry had established strong ties with the Emerson family. Other than his own sisters, Lidian Emerson was one of the few women with whom he had ever shared a deep friendship. He appreciated such intimacy. Nevertheless, he rarely admitted to any longing for romance or marriage. Especially after his unsuccessful proposal to Ellen Sewall, it seemed that Henry Thoreau preferred the bachelor's life. As he put it, "I have given myself to nature."

And indeed he had. In the years that followed his Walden retreat, Henry would return to live with his own family in Concord. For a while, he would make pencils. Later he would find employment as a surveyor, but these were minor distractions. What really mattered were his walks through the wildlands around Concord—usually for two to four hours each afternoon.

Often the candle in Henry's bedroom was the only one burning in the house, as he wrote detailed notes of his ramblings in his journal late at night. When the moon was full, he often stayed out until the sun came up. "The woodland paths are never seen to such advantage as in a moonlit night," he

Concord, Massachusetts, in winter

wrote in his journal in June 1851. "At night you are sure to hear what is still awake. . . . The wind blows, the river flows, without resting. There lies Fair Haven Lake, indistinguishable from fallen sky... Instead of flowers underfoot, stars overhead."

While others sought refuge by the warmth of their fires, Henry loved to venture out in the snow. To be awake and alert was to be alive, and Henry found such weather invigorating. Henry relished his role as an "inspector of snowstorms."

One day a perfect snowflake landed, like a tiny silver star, on his coat sleeve. Henry watched the wings of the six-sided crystal melt. "What a world we live in! where myriads of these little discs, so beautiful to the most prying eye, are whirled down on some traveler's coat," he wrote. "The meadow mouse shoves them aside in his gallery, the school-boy casts them in his snowball, . . . the woodman's sled glides smoothly over them." But Henry took the time to observe these snowflakes which he described as "glorious spangles, the sweeping of heaven's floor."

While journal entries like this one reflected Henry's love of land and language, others were more scientific. He spent several years learning about the flowers—where they grew, when they bloomed— and carefully logged this information in his notes.

Thoreau studied and appreciated the beauty of all the plants around him, such as this pink lady's slipper.

Once he knew the flowers, he studied the grasses. Then the mosses. Then the mushrooms. For Henry Thoreau, the discoveries waiting to be made in his own backyard were as endless as the forests below the ridges of Mount Katahdin.

A REPORTER OF NATURE

CHAPTER FIVE

*. . . If one advances confi-
dently in the direction of
his dreams, and endeavors
to live the life which he has imagined, he will meet with a suc-
cess unexpected in common hours.*

—Henry David Thoreau

As Henry had discovered in New York City, the writer's life was not an easy one as far as making a living was concerned. Even widely published writers of his time such as Edgar Allen Poe were poorly paid for their labors. Recognizing this, Henry decided to find other ways of making a living. In doing so, he chose not to worry about selling his

MIST

HOW-ANCHORED CLOUD,
NEWFOUNDLAND AIR,
FOUNTAIN-HEAD AND SOURCE OF RIVERS,
DEW-CLOTH, DREAM-DRAPERY,
AND NAPKIN SPREAD FOR FAYS;
DRIFTING MEADOW OF THE AIR,
WHERE BLOOM THE DAISIED BANKS AND VIOLETS
AND IN WHOSE FENNY LABYRINTHS
THE BITTERN BOOMS AND HERON WADES;
SPIRIT OF LAKES AND SEAS AND RIVERS,
BEAR ONLY PERFUME AND THE SCENT
OF HEALING HERBS TO JUST MEN'S FIELDS.

HENRY D. THOREAU.

Thoreau's poem, "Mist," as it appeared in print in 1880

work, opting instead for the freedom to write what he pleased.

Still, Henry wanted to get his work published. And when that opportunity came, he was as anxious and hopeful as any young writer might have been. In the summer of 1849, a positive review in the New York Tribune increased his expectations for A Week on the Concord and Merrimack Rivers, his first book.

It was only after numerous rejections that Henry had been able to find a willing publisher for the book. Even then, he had been asked to put up one hundred dollars of his own money to cover part of the printing costs. "I was obliged to manufacture a thousand dollars worth of pencils . . . in order to pay back the hundred-dollar debt," Henry later wrote. It was an investment that he believed would pay off.

So did Henry's friend Bronson Alcott, another Concord writer and father of Louisa May Alcott. "It seems likely to become a popular book with our people here," Alcott said, but his optimistic prediction proved false. By 1853, only 219 out of one thousand printed copies had been sold. Fortunately for Henry, his pencils sold better than his books did, and he was able to pay the printer for the remaining copies.

Amos Bronson Alcott

Soon a man arrived at Henry's door with a wagon full of boxes. "They are more substantial than fame, as my back knows which has borne them up two flights of stairs," Henry wrote after unloading his books. "I have now a library of nearly nine hundred volumes, over seven hundred of which I wrote myself."

If fame had been his main ambition, Henry Thoreau would have had good reason to be discouraged over the response to his first book. Even those neighbors who had heard of his book still thought of Henry as an odd-job man who worked occasionally as a surveyor. Emerson and others appreciated his writing, but they were beginning to wonder if Henry Thoreau would ever find his audience.

Audience or no audience, Henry was still intent on exploring the wildlands around Concord, and he was still determined to describe his experiences. Even though his writings were often imaginative and poetic, Henry described himself as a reporter in nature. And a reporter's primary responsibilities were to stay alert, observe the world, and record the experience.

The experiences he recorded in the pages of his journal would later provide the raw material for essays such as the ones that appeared in Walden, his second book, which was published in 1854. There

WALDEN;

OR,

LIFE IN THE WOODS.

By HENRY D. THOREAU,

AUTHOR OF "A WEEK ON THE CONCORD AND MERRIMACK RIVERS."

The opening page to Walden by Henry David Thoreau.
His book is still considered one of the most important
works of American literature.

On the shore of Walden Pond, a simple mound of
stones commemorates the life of Henry David Thoreau.
The memorial is located near the site of his cabin.

would be no need to make pencils to pay off printing debts this time. Several positive reviews would help boost sales to two thousand.

In Walden, Henry made his case for personal freedom, for the value of a simple life, and for the solace to be found in nature. Few of his neighbors would have guessed that Henry Thoreau's words would inspire readers for many years to come. Even Henry might have been surprised to see how the words he wrote at Walden took root, like windblown seeds, all over the world.

As it turned out, Henry would not live long enough to see the book's second printing. He would never fully recover from the cough that plagued him during the winter of 1860. In May 1861, his friends convinced him to travel west to Minnesota, hoping that the inland air would rid him of his incessant cough, but it was too late for a cure.

By late fall of 1861, he was too sick to venture outdoors. Most of the time he was unable to sleep. Nevertheless, he entertained visitors with his usual sense of humor. One day, a stern and very religious aunt asked him if he'd made his peace with God. Henry informed her that he did not know that he and God had ever quarreled.

As his condition worsened, it was suggested that he take opiates so that he could sleep, but Henry

Henry David Thoreau

refused to cloud his thoughts with such medications. He had too much work to do. He would spend his final days organizing the essays and journal entries that resulted in several travel books such as *The Maine Woods*, an account of his adventures in the wilds of New England. Along with two other books on Canada and Cape Cod, it would be published shortly after his death, which came quietly on the morning of May 6, 1862.

Several days later, his friends and family gathered in a Concord church to hear Ralph Waldo Emerson, among others, bid Henry David Thoreau farewell. "Wherever there is knowledge, wherever there is virtue, wherever there is beauty," Emerson said, Henry "will find a home."

FOR FURTHER READING

Amdur, Richard. *Wilderness Preservation*. New York: Chelsea House Publishers, 1993.

Challand, Helen J. *Vanishing Forests*. Chicago: Childrens Press, 1991.

Faber, Doris. *Nature and the Environment*. New York: Scribner, 1991.

Hirsch, S. Carl. *Guardians of Tomorrow: Pioneers in Ecology*. New York: Viking Press, 1971.

Keene, Ann T. *Earthkeepers: Observers and Protectors of Nature*. New York: Oxford University Press, 1994.

Miller, Douglas. *Henry David Thoreau*. New York: Facts on File, 1991.

Reef, Catherine, *Henry David Thoreau: A Neighbor to Nature*. New York: Twenty-First Century Books, 1992.

Ring, Elizabeth. *Henry David Thoreau: In Step with Nature*. Brookfield, Conn.: Millbrook Press, 1993.

INDEX

ABOUT THE AUTHOR

Peter Anderson has worked as a river guide, carpenter, newspaper reporter, writing teacher, editor, and wilderness ranger. He has written ten books for young readers on topics related to nature, Native Americans, and the history of the American West. Currently, he lives in Salt Lake City, Utah.